RATTLE YOUR BONES

Skeleton Drawing Fun

by David Clemesha and Andrea Griffing Zimmerman

SCHOLASTIC INC.
New York Toronto London Auckland Sydney

Photo Credits

ISBN 0-590-45263-0

12 11 10 9   9/9

Printed in the U.S.A.   23

First Scholastic printing, October 1991

Skeleton Drawing Fun

To Alex

CONTENTS

Chapter 1

FROM STICK FIGURE TO SKELETON

Can you draw a stick figure like this?

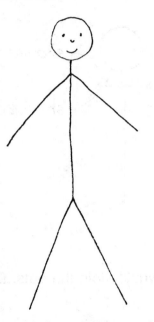

Of course you can!

Then you can easily change your stick figure into a scary skeleton.

Find some drawing paper and a pencil.

Start by drawing the head and spine.

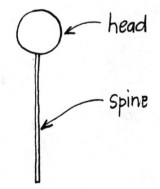

Add a shoulder line with two dots for shoulders.

See how there's a neck now?

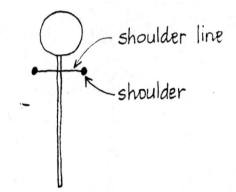

Put dots for the elbows and wrists. Join the dots. Draw in the finger bones.

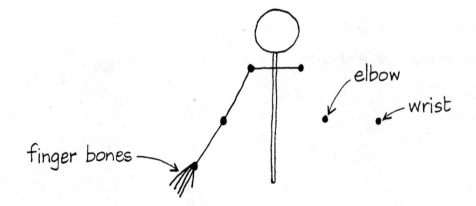

Draw in an oval for your skeleton's rib cage. Make it hang from your skeleton's shoulder line. Draw in lines sloping downwards to show your skeleton's ribs.

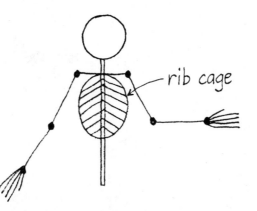

To make your skeleton's hips, draw a square. Put dots at the hips. Put dots where you want the knees and ankles. Join the dots. Draw in the foot bones.

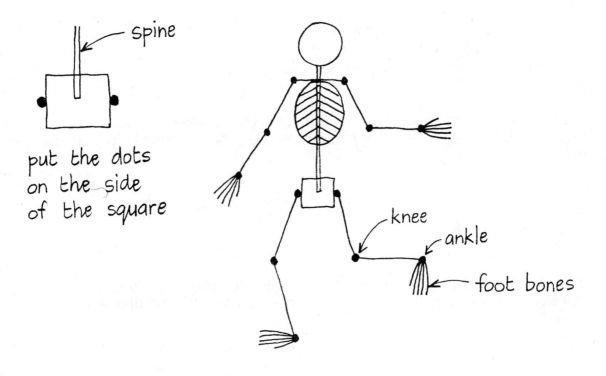

spine

put the dots
on the side
of the square

knee

ankle

foot bones

To turn the head of your stick figure into a skull, draw an oval. Draw two dark ovals for eye sockets. Then draw a dark triangle for a nose cavity.

make your skeleton's
head oval or
egg-shaped

Add to the skull some teeth and cheekbones.

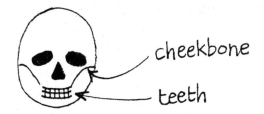

In order to make your skeleton look real, change the lines of the arms and legs into bones. Arms, legs, fingers, and toes are "long bones." Their shape is similar to this:

It is a long middle piece with a bump on each end. You can add to your skeleton very easily by making double lines and changing the dots into bumps.

See how easy it is to go from your first stick figure to a scary skeleton.

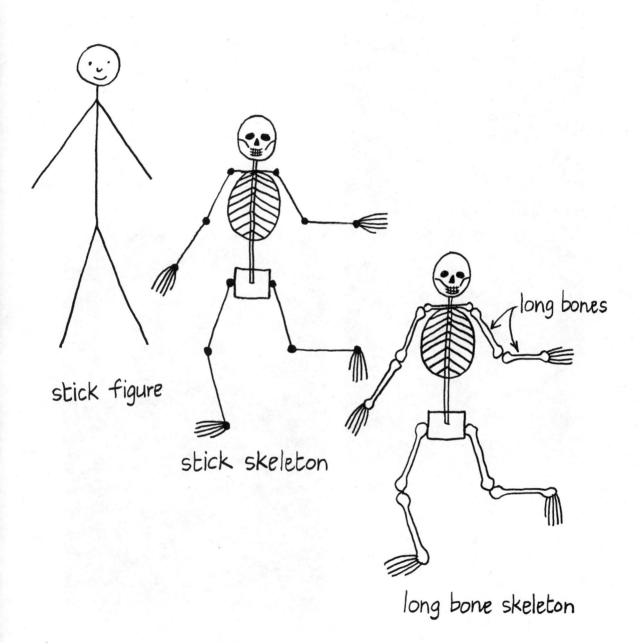

stick figure

stick skeleton

long bones

long bone skeleton

Here are photographs of a real skeleton and a skull.

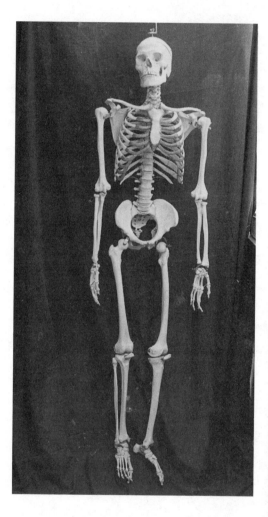

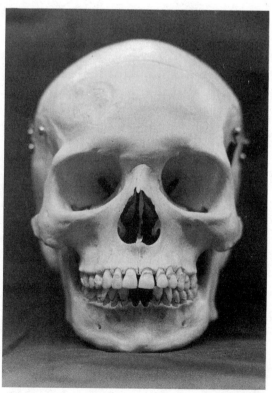

Chapter 2

DRAWING YOUR SKELETON FROM THE SIDE

Drawing your skeleton from the side is as easy as drawing it from the front.

Follow these steps:

Here is a drawing of a stick figure seen from the side.

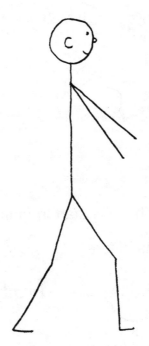

The big difference when drawing a person or skeleton from the side is that the shoulders overlap. That means that the arms start from the same dot.

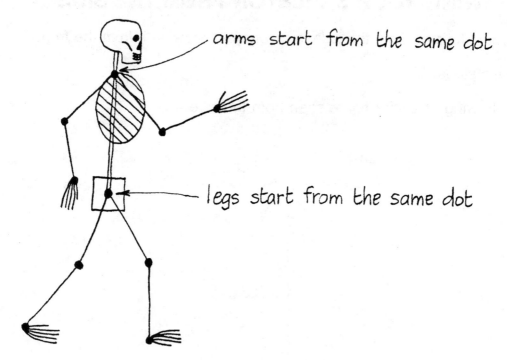

arms start from the same dot

legs start from the same dot

The same goes for the hips. The legs start from the same dot.

Now draw a head and spine as before.

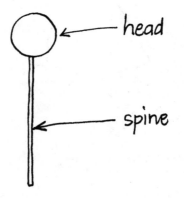

head

spine

Draw dots where the shoulders, elbows, and wrists are. There should be just one dot for the shoulders. Connect the dots.

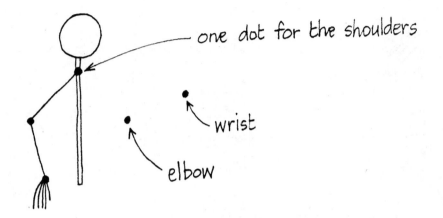

Add the oval for the rib cage. Make the lines slope downwards for the rib cage. Don't worry if you draw on top of the arms. Your drawing will still look all right.

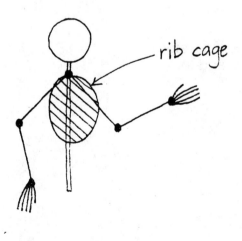

Then draw in the hip box and dots for the hips, knees, and ankles. Connect the dots. Are the legs coming from the same hip dot?

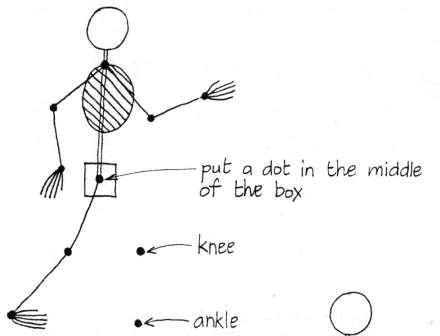

put a dot in the middle of the box

knee

ankle

Add foot and hand bones. As before, you can change the arms and legs into long bones.

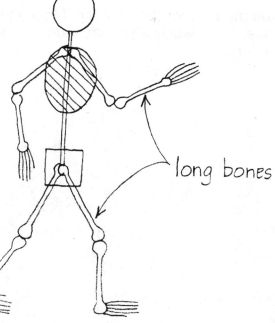

long bones

Adding details to the skull of your skeleton can create a more scary and lifelike skeleton.

A skull from the side looks different than from the front. Change your stick figure's head into a skull by following these steps:

Draw an oval this way:

Draw a rectangle this way:

Now put them together.

Erase the unnecessary lines.

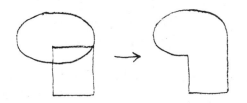

Now add an oval eye socket and a triangular nose cavity.

Add teeth and a cheekbone like this:

Now you have a skeleton's head seen from the side that should scare anybody!

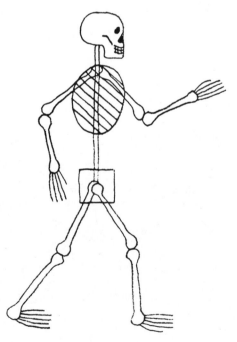

Here's a photograph of a human skeleton from the side.

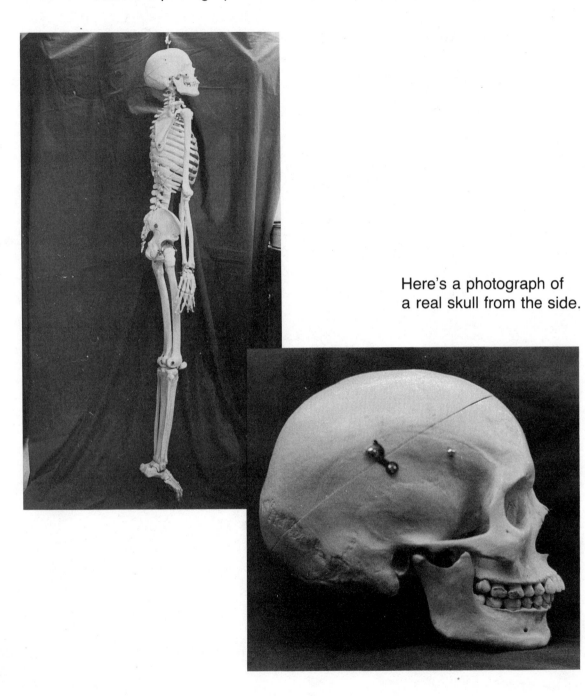

Here's a photograph of
a real skull from the side.

Chapter 3

DRAWING YOUR SKELETON IN DIFFERENT POSITIONS

One of the ways to make a fun skeleton drawing is to draw it doing something.

Try drawing lots of stick figures in different positions.

Do any of the ones you have drawn look like they might be doing something in particular? Adding minor details can give your figures more personality.

It's fun to play around with stick figures.

Anything your stick figure does you can also make a skeleton do.

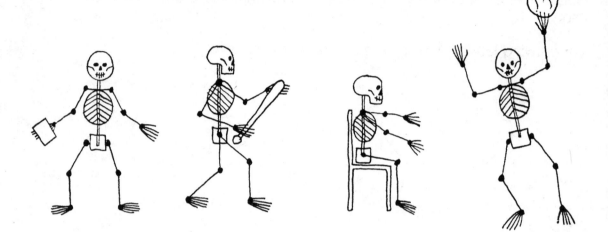

Here's another idea to help you draw your skeleton doing things.

Have a friend lean against a chair.
Draw a stick figure quickly.

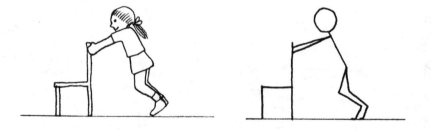

From your stick figure develop a skeleton as you did before.

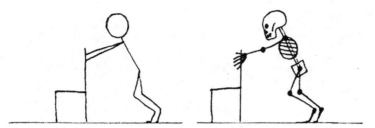

Have your friend act as if he or she is playing a favorite sport, climbing a big tree, or whatever you want to draw a skeleton doing.

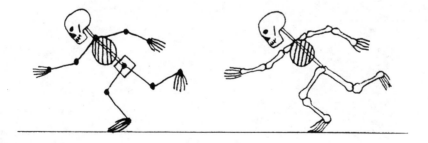

Chapter 4

USING PHOTOGRAPHS TO DRAW SKELETONS

Photographs can give you still more ideas for drawing interesting skeletons.

Find some old magazines. Look through the pages to find a picture that you like. Take a piece of tracing paper and tape it down over that picture. Taping the tracing paper down keeps it from moving. Lightly trace the outline of the person in the picture.

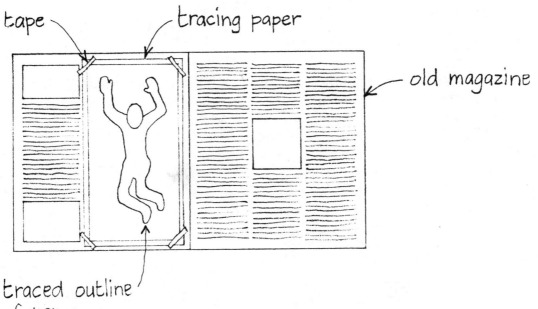

tape

tracing paper

old magazine

traced outline of person

Draw in the skull and spine.

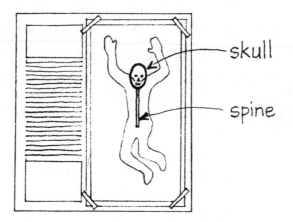

skull

spine

Draw dots where the shoulders are and connect them with a line. In this example, notice how the shoulder line is partly hidden.

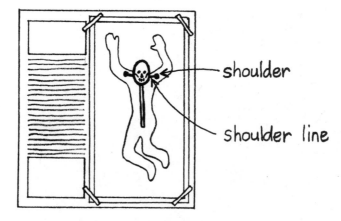

shoulder

shoulder line

Add the dots for the elbows and wrists and connect them with a line. Draw in the hand bones.

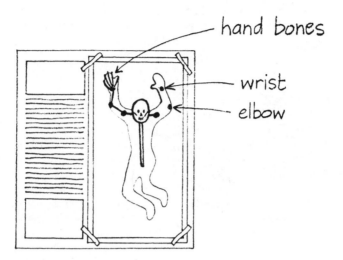

Draw in the oval rib cage. Remember, the rib cage touches the shoulder line. In this example, the head is in front of the shoulder line so part of the rib cage is hidden.

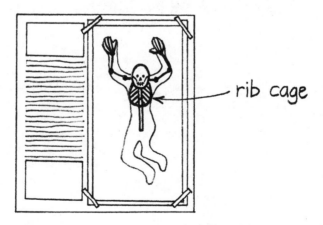

Draw in a square for the hip area. Make sure you put dots on this square for the top of the leg bones.
Draw in dots for the knees and ankles.
Join the top of each leg bone to the knee bone and the ankle bone. And then draw in the foot bones.

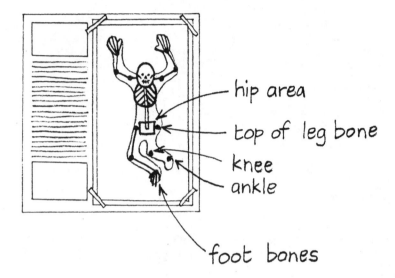

hip area

top of leg bone

knee

ankle

foot bones

Untape the tracing paper and look at the skeleton you've created.

tracing paper

Erase the outline carefully so you are left with just the skeleton drawing on your tracing paper.

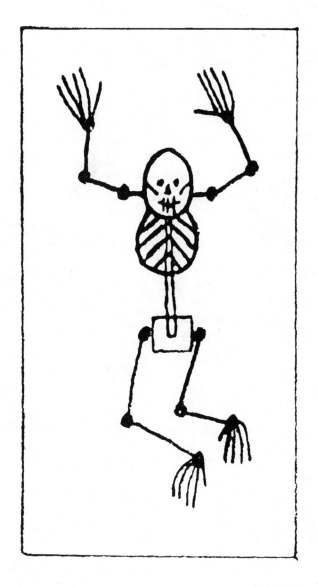

Chapter 5

MAKING A COPY OF YOUR SKELETON

If you want to make a more finished drawing of a skeleton, copy the skeleton you now have on tracing paper onto drawing paper. Here's how you do it without having to start a drawing of your skeleton all over again.

Turn your skeleton tracing over. With the side of your pencil shade the back side of your tracing.

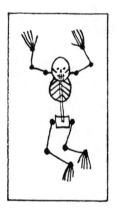

front side

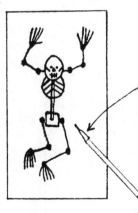

back side

use a pencil to shade the back side of the tracing paper

Turn your tracing paper back over to the front side again. Tape a piece of drawing paper to your drawing board or table. On top of this drawing paper tape down your skeleton tracing.

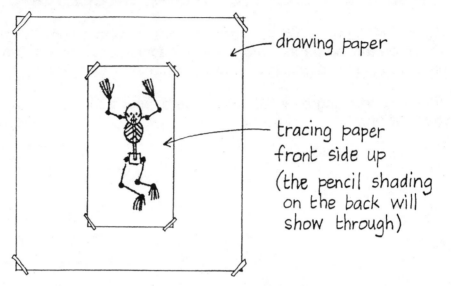

drawing paper

tracing paper front side up
(the pencil shading on the back will show through)

With a pencil that is not too sharp (you might rip the tracing paper if it is), press down carefully as you draw on top of the lines and dots of your skeleton.

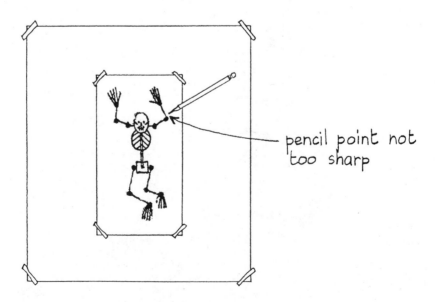

pencil point not too sharp

Untape your tracing paper and look at the copy you've made on the drawing paper. To make your skeleton stand out use a felt-tip pen, crayons, or perhaps black ink, applied with a brush. This will sharpen the fuzzy, smudgy lines.

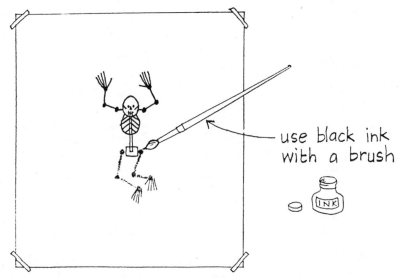

use black ink with a brush

After putting another coating of pencil on the back of your tracing paper, place it in different positions on another sheet, or the same sheet, of drawing paper.
You can make copies of your skeleton wherever you wish.

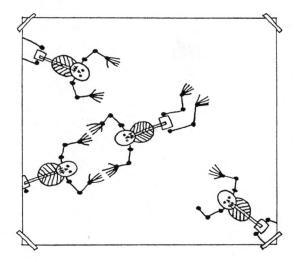

Chapter 6

SKELETONS IN ART

Throughout history, artists have made pictures, designs, and sculptures using skeletons.

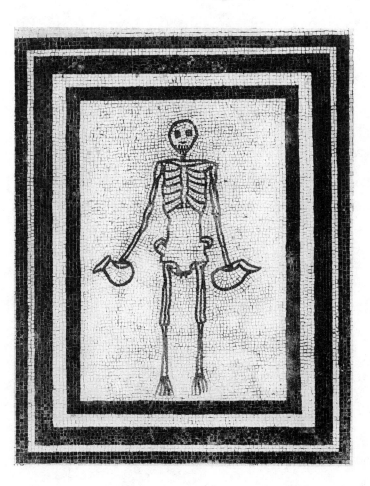

This skeleton was done by a Roman artist over 2,000 years ago in Pompeii. It is a mosaic design. A mosaic artist makes a picture out of hundreds of little colored pieces of glass, stone, or marble.

This woodblock print was made about two hundred years ago by a Japanese artist named Kawanabe Kyosai. As you can see, he had lots of fun drawing skeletons in silly and unusual positions.

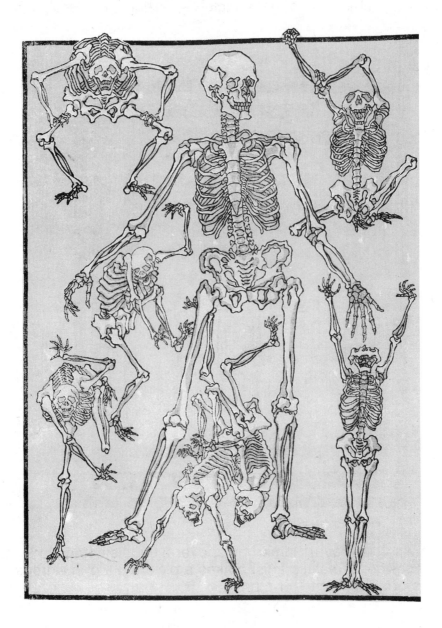

Vincent van Gogh, the famous Dutch artist who lived over a hundred years ago, painted this skeleton puffing on a cigarette. Wouldn't this make a great anti-smoking poster?

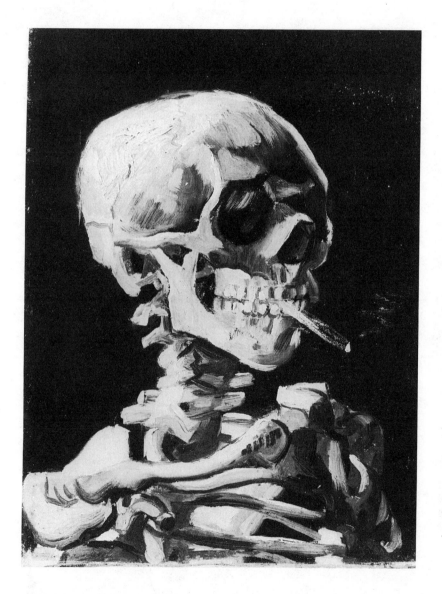

Leonardo da Vinci, the man who painted the Mona Lisa, was a brilliant artist. He took dead bodies apart so that he could draw their skeletons. His knowledge of every bone and muscle in the human face made him able to paint the mysterious smile for which his Mona Lisa painting is known.

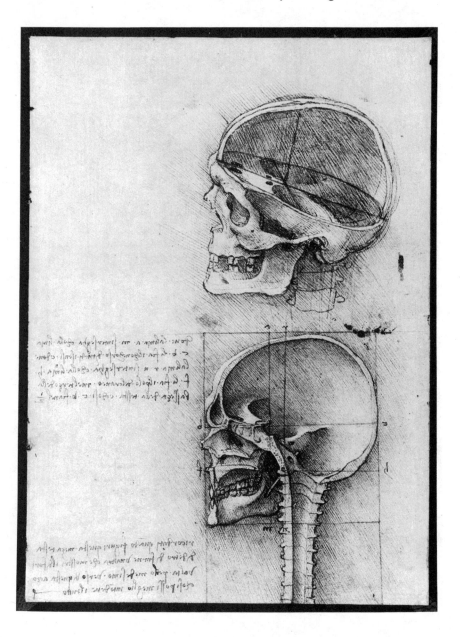

Hans Holbein the Younger was a German artist who put together a book called *The Dance of Death*, which was published about 450 years ago. This book contained 41 illustrations of skeletons in everyday situations. In this picture a skeleton is leading an old man to the doctor.

Mexican artist José Guadalupe Posada made this print about a hundred years ago of a popular Mexican holiday.

The Day of the Dead is a two-day celebration in Mexico on November 1 and 2. All over Mexico, the people happily welcome home the spirits of the dead. For this festival, special bread and candies are made in the shapes of skeletons and skulls. There are also many skeleton toys and decorations that children can buy at this time.

Chapter 7

OTHER ART PROJECTS WITH SKELETONS

There are many other things you can do with skeletons.
Here are some ideas:

1. Your own skeleton

Materials you'll need:
a pencil and a black felt-tip pen
a large sheet of paper
(This must be as long and as
wide as your body. If you can't
find one big piece of paper, you
could tape together newsprint or
cut apart grocery sacks.)

Get a friend to help you. Then follow these steps:

Tape the large sheet of paper to a smooth, hard floor such as the floor in
your kitchen or bathroom.

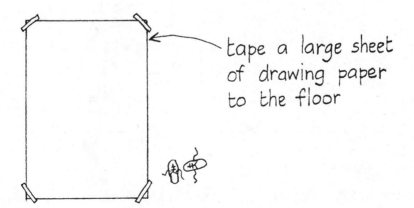

tape a large sheet
of drawing paper
to the floor

Lie down, facing upwards, on the paper.

Have your friend make a line with a pencil around the outside of your body.

Fill in this outlined shape with skeleton bones.

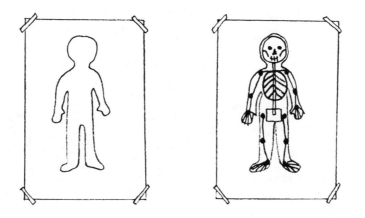

Help your friend do this project, too. Create a life-sized skeleton from her or his body.

You can use a doll to develop a skeleton from its outline, too.

Just follow the same procedure as for a life-sized drawing.
Draw an outline of the doll on a sheet of paper.
Be sure to hold the doll steady.
Then draw the skeleton in this outline.

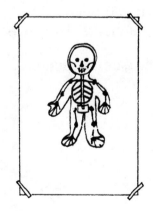

2. Stick skeletons:

Materials you'll need:
a box of toothpicks
(or uncooked spaghetti,
or sticks from the yard)
glue
a sheet of construction paper
(black would be a great choice)

Arrange the pieces to make a skeleton. You'll probably have to break some of the toothpicks in half when you make the skull and the hip area.

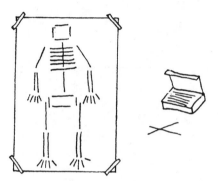

When you have all the toothpicks arranged just as you want them, pick up one carefully. Using tweezers can help.

Apply glue to each tip.

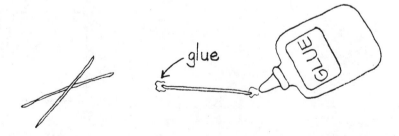

Put each toothpick back in the position from where you took it.
Add glue to each toothpick until your whole skeleton is glued down to the paper.

Here's another toothpick idea:

After you are sure your toothpick skeleton has dried thoroughly, put a piece of paper over it, and then gently rub over the paper with a crayon. The ridges made by the toothpicks will push into the back of the paper and a drawing will appear. This also can be done with sticks and uncooked spaghetti.

3. Pipe-cleaner skeletons

Materials you'll need:
pipe cleaners
scissors
glue
construction paper

Bend the pipe cleaners. Cut them into the sizes you need.
Glue them down on the sheet of construction paper.

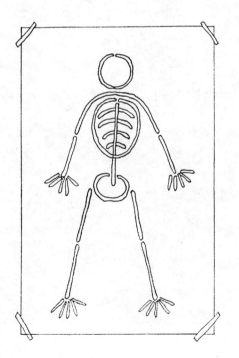

4. Ghostly skeletons

Materials you'll need:
white chalk
black construction paper

Look at some of the skeletons you've already drawn. Redraw them with white chalk on black construction paper. It will make them look spooky.

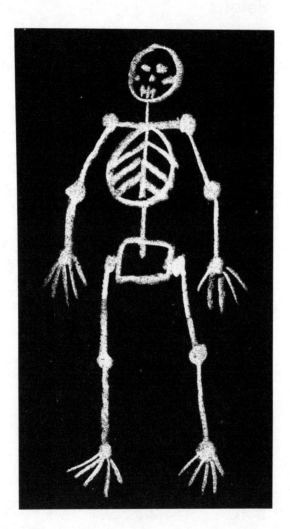

5. Scratched skeletons

Materials you'll need:
crayons
nail
sheet of drawing paper
paint

Cover the sheet of drawing paper with four or five layers of different-colored crayons. Completely cover the crayon layers with a thick layer of poster paint. Make sure that you let this paint dry completely!
Scratch the paint with a nail and draw a skeleton. The colored crayon will show through.

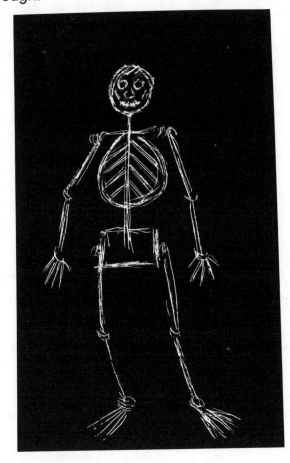

scratch with a nail

6. Decorating skulls

Materials you'll need:
paper
pencils
crayons
or whatever you want to use

Draw pictures of skulls and then decorate them with headdresses, hats, or anything else you think would be silly or unusual.

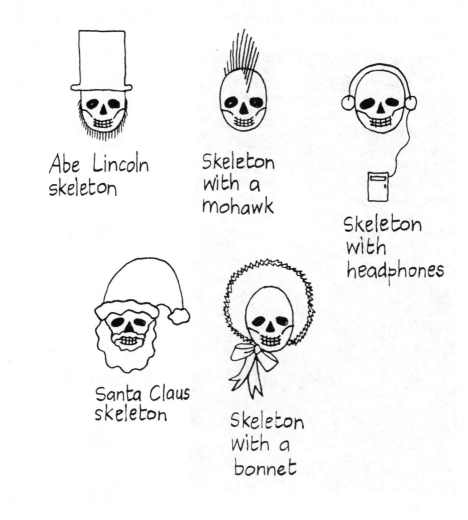

Abe Lincoln skeleton

Skeleton with a mohawk

Skeleton with headphones

Santa Claus skeleton

Skeleton with a bonnet

7. Skeleton writing

Materials you'll need:
cardboard that's easy to cut
scissors
pencil
drawing paper

Draw three bones of different lengths on a piece of cardboard. Cut them out and make a stencil.

cardboard

cut out
the shapes

stencil

Use your bone stencil to give spooky feelings to words by writing them in long bones.

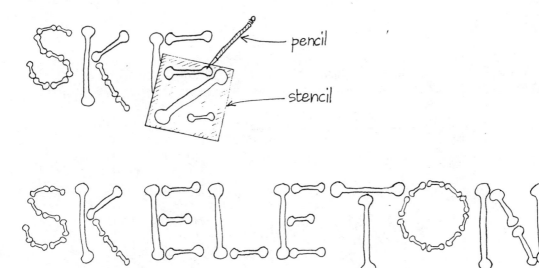

pencil

stencil

Another way is to lightly draw the word you want to write.

Darkly draw over this word in long bones. Use your imagination. O's can be skulls!

8. Spooky skeleton scenes

Materials you'll need:
paper
pencils
markers

Draw a skeleton on a sheet of paper. Build an eerie scene around your skeleton. Draw in coffins, ghosts, haunted mansions, owls, and graveyards.

Here are some spooky things to choose from and use in your drawings.

9. Silly skeletons

Materials you'll need:
markers
pencils
paints
paper

Things that people do can look very silly and weird when drawn with skeletons instead.

Draw any kind of scene, like the circus, underwater diving, or motorcycle riding, and draw skeletons instead of people.

 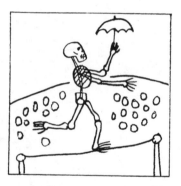

10. Moving skeletons

Materials you'll need:
lightweight cardboard
a nail
string
scissors
pencil

Draw the bones of a skeleton on cardboard that is easy to cut (such as an old tissue box).

Cut out the bones.

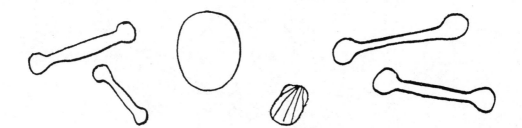

Make small holes with the nail where the bones attach.

Tie the pieces together with string.

You can position this skeleton in a number of ways or just make it jump around.

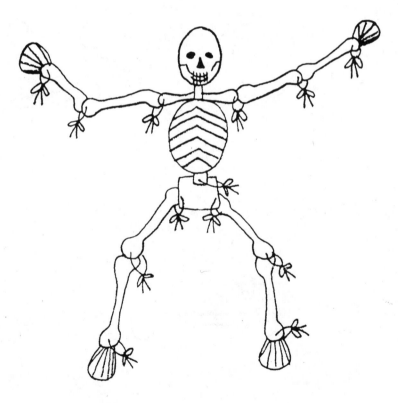

11. "SKULL-pture" rock art

Materials you'll need:
a clean rock (any size)
a black marker pen

marker

Use a black marker to draw on the rock the eyes, nose, teeth, and cheek-bones of a skull.

12. Pirate flags

Materials you'll need:
piece of white or black cloth
white or black paper
a black marker pen or black paint
white paint

Use a piece of white or black cloth or paper to make the skull and cross-bones, or Jolly Roger pirate flag.
On black cloth or paper use white paint.
On white cloth or paper use black marker pen or black paint.
Tie your finished flag to a stick or hang it on your wall.

stick

58

13. Airheads and Eggheads

Materials you'll need:
balloons
eggs
marker pen

Blow up some balloons or ask your parents to hard boil some eggs.
Draw skulls on the balloons or eggs.
Make lots of Airheads or Eggheads.

Skeletons are around you every day at home and at school. They are just covered up by skin and clothes! You can draw them out and have

FUN WITH SKELETONS!